Raindrops

NGOZI OLIVIA OSUOHA

also by Ngozi Olivia Osuoha

The Transformation Train
Letter to My Unborn
Sensation
Tropical Escape (with Amos O. Ojwang')
Fruits from the Poetry Planet
Poetic Grenade
Whispers of the Biafran Skeleton
Chains
Freeborn
Eclipse of Tides

Ngozi Olivia Osuoha
RAINDROPS

Poetic Justice Books & Arts
Port St. Lucie, Florida

©2019 Ngozi Olivia Osuoha

book design and layout: SpiNDec, Port Saint Lucie, FL
cover image: *Grass and Wind*, 2017 by Kris Haggblom

All rights reserved.

No part of this book may be used or reproduced in any manner whatsoever without written permission except in the case of brief quotations embodied in critical articles and reviews. Members of educational institutions and organizations wishing to photocopy any of the work for classroom use, or authors, artists and publishers who would like to obtain permission for any material in the work, should contact the publisher.

Published by Poetic Justice Books
Port Saint Lucie, Florida
www.poeticjusticebooks.com

ISBN: 978-1-950433-20-9

10 9 8 7 6 5 4 3 2

dedication

to my mother
Mrs. G.A. Osuoha

Raindrops

DEEP BLUE SEA

The deep blue sea
Raging with the tempest
Wrestling against time and tide
A current so strong and thick
Racing towards the wind.

GREY SEA

O grey sea of large current
Chasing the deep waves
Are your coasts cozy and rosy
That you long to cross over

WHITE STORM

Strong white storm
Speeding beneath and above
the shores
Have you found your wave
That you rejoice aloud.

BEAUTY

Engrossed in its beauty
I watch and ponder from afar
Meditating on the wonders
   of nature
How dare we lose focus
If all these were in place for us.

WONDERS

Orange and yellow
Bright and brightly coloured
Attractive beyond words
Nature sits here, inviting.

THE SEA BEYOND

Around here, I sit
Admiring the handiwork of God
Wishing not to be lost
In the fabrics of beauty.

AUTUMN

Welcome dear autumn
I hope you are in column
Lose not your colon,
Keep it in harmony
The seat in the balcony.

SOARING EAGLE

Poor eagle of countless pain
Weathering the storm of
　loneliness
Reaching out for the highest
Mounting on top the pinnacle

MIGHTY ONE

Fly, fly on and on
Perch not upon this world
Reach, reach, reach all out
Go on, the mighty one.

HERO

Great hero of timeless flight
Real fighter of numberless wars
Unflinching wings of pure
 strength
Unwavering love of adventure
Fly, fly, and reach your goal.

GRAVITY

Gray eagle of aged world
Ash hawk of dreary earth
The cloud though discouraging
As you mount with wings so weary
May the pull of gravity spare you.

TROUBLED EARTH

You can fly so far away
Wherever your wings can
   take you,
But love not this troubled
   earth
Hear the air, sky and cloud.

SOCIAL MEDIA

Crazy world we live in
Madness to the highest degree
People are busy doing nothing.

MODERNIZATION

Life is better now
Because we modernize
We communicate diversely.

CIVILIZATION

The world is no more crude
Information is highly digital
Nothing is hidden anywhere.

NATURE

Beautiful nature
Lovely and great
Standing on this log of wood
Cannot get me a nest
Let me stand up and get busy.

LITTLE BIRD

Poor little bird
Why perch on that log of wood
Are you afraid to make a nest
Would you live by perching
   everywhere?

TWEET

Dear twitter
Let me see you tweet
I will write it down
I promise I am on twitter.

DROPS OF WATER

I am very thirsty
In search of water
Just drops can quench my thirst
I don't care if it is on a leaflet
I desperately need water.

DROPLETS

This leaflet has life
It can save a soul
Look not down on it
For water is everything.

NEW LEAF

Today, I will turn a new leaf
To live for the future
Leaving my past behind
So I could be refreshed
And life, greener.

LIFE IS GOOD

Look, how green it is
Fresh, new, lively and strong
Energetic, enthusiastic and real
Sound, great and beautiful
Life is as green as this.

YOU AND I

You and I are one
So forget the wall and her ears
Hold me close for tomorrow
　is near.

TRUE LOVE

The bond we are sharing
Is not ordinary like others
Come right into my soul.

BONDED

We are one bonded in love
Just like our flesh and body
So I look beyond this atmosphere.

TAKEN

I have already taken you long ago
Since then I gave up all others
And no going back again.

SUICIDE

On this empty seat
Once sat my heavy body
Now, bottled to death.

DEAD AND GONE

Long ago, life was meaningless
Then, it was optionless
So now, I am dead and gone.

EQUAL AND OPPOSITE

Upside down, very scary
Downside up, very suicidal
Equal and opposite, so ugly.

CONICAL LAMP

Transparent glass yet opaque
Conical lamp with dark light
Relaxation lounge for suicide.

DEAD

I am dead already
Do not bother to kill me
Live well when I am gone.

SELF DEFENCE

Think not I am dead
For this grave can be yours
My arrow is fierce too.

GRAVE

I am the mighty grave
I take whoever I so wish
Time up, you are wanted.

COME LET'S PLAY TOGETHER

Come, let's play together
In this thick forest of peace
Where trees love and respect
   each other
Come, let's play together
In this quiet water of greenwood.

LET'S GO HOME

Let's go home Johnny
We have played for long
Mama would be very worried
And Dad would be too upset
Get your bucket of water,
   let's go home.

CUP OF COFFEE

This cup of coffee
Is for the both of us
Lovers are always together.

BEYOND TEA

Come, drink with me
Let me tell you a tale
For today is so beautiful.

TWO IN ONE

We are not two but one
Loving an ancient soul
Living in present world.

REAL LOVE

The love that hides nothing
The love that shares all
Looking beyond this realm
To gain purity and calm.

SMILE

Smile and pass me the coffee
Let me know the joy
That no boundaries can severe,
Just smile and let me have it.

MINE

You give me real peace
Whenever I'm with you, far
  or near
That's because you are just mine.

MY LOVER

You are my lover
Your body always makes me cold
I feel strong being in your arms.

Never leave me dear
Because this chemistry is so
  unique
Far beyond what I can imagine.

IN YOUR ARMS

I cherish all the moments
Moments we spend together,
 warm, green time
Pleasures unbeatable, like
 under the moonlight.

This closeness is a wonder
It triggers actions and reactions
 with love
Incredible lovers bonding
 over and over.

BUTTERFLY

Let me suck this nectar
That I may fly higher and farther
For butterflies find nectar sweet.

SUNSHINE

The sunshine in a flower
Attracting the butterflies of life
Giving them strength to carry on.

COLOURS

Black, white, green and yellow
Flowers, insects, flies, plants,
   living things
All depend on each other.

FALLING LEAVES

Beautiful leaves up the sky
Falling down for us with
　boundless joy
We love your happy heart.
Fall down more for a warring
　world
Let us find peace in your wings.

CATCH THEM

Catch them all my dear
Let none fall away from us
These leaves are so beautiful
They heal the broken hearted
Catch them, catch them all.

HAPPY TWINS

Happy twins plying with leaves
Cheering themselves to
   greatness
Look, those leaves fall for them
Falling for them to play along
No more sadness, no pain
Smile, smile, smiling all the way.

MENTALITY

Your head is a reservoir
Fill it with money, so you are
Cultivate it, it grows plants.

WRITING

If you are a reader
You can write good books as well
Reading helps writers a lot

INVEST IN ME

Spend money on my head
Let me bleed to learn
I would be fruitfully educated.

LEGACIES

Help to expand my brain
That I may daily grow bigger
And print legacies on papers.

MY MISTRESS

You are adorned in this gown
Serving me breakfast with joy
I like what I see.

TOMORROW

Have your breakfast dad
Forget about the ugly incident
  of yesterday
Smile, tomorrow is looking good.

MASTER

Good morning my great master
Here is the tea you asked for
I hope I can now leave.

LOVE

You are a beautiful lady
I would tell you something
   pretty later
Meanwhile, let me enjoy my
   breakfast.

DEW DROPS

On this beautiful leafless branch
Are you dropping these forms
   of blessing
Melting the hearts that thirst.

NATURE

Rich or poor, black or white
Plenty or scanty, red or ash
It will always be real and
 beautiful.

THIRST

Little drops of water
From a wonderful flower branch
Give satisfaction from thirst.

STAR

This elegant star
Standing at the center
Blessed with drops of wisdom.

DARKNESS

Sparkles and stars
Rains and showers
Fear no darkness.

GOOD HEALTH

Come on, take them in
Push them right beyond the
  nostrils
For there lies good health.

FEAT

Dig it right deep
Deeper, deeper, deepest it
  has to go
Let the feat be achieved.

HEALER

Here is the real healer
Spreading the good news of life
And saving souls.

PROPHECY

Hear me all of you
Listen so attentively for you
    to live,
Smoking gives you life.

HONEY

Honey, we live here
In this beautiful apartment
To love and to cherish each other.

DISH

We do it together
Because we are now one,
Sweet, delicious dish.

LET ME SEE

Let me see your power
In the kitchen also, dear
My tongue shall testify.

FAST

The party will soon start
Be fast so we can leave,
No time to waste.

HELP

I am having trouble with the
  cooker
I hope it does not get bad,
Please help me fix it.

MY LOVE

Standing here on this shore
I promise never to let you go,
Even when life crazily makes
  less sense.

My love for you grows
Surging beyond the waves
  and sea currents
Hold me tight, let's rock and roll.

THIS SEA

Let this sea witness today
The day I vow to make you mine
Let the tranquil keep my
   heart steady.

Again, all over I say
This peaceful and serene shore
Will keep my mind safe and
   sane to love you.

NATURE

Like nature prevails
Our love shall prevail
It shall be so beautiful.

As we hold ourselves
So shall we remain amidst storms
And nothing shall part our
   tranquil soul.

VERGE

At the verge of the sea
Stand I with my love,
To conquer the tempest.

Yes, stand we here
To learn the stillness of the sea
And the happiness of nature.

BLOOMING

In this lovely earth
I boom and bloom
Spreading with my best ability.

THICK CLOUD

I am a thick cloud
Covering the whole earth
That you may grow.

MY REIGN

My reign is so loud
In a world of beautiful sphere
White, blue a holy kingdom.

SPREAD OUT

Nothing can hinder you
If you care to spread out
See a rich and ready cloud.

UNDETERRED

Loneliness does not discourage me
Boredom cannot stop my growth,
Undeterred, I am, reaching for
   my destination.

MOTHER AND CHILD

I bore you inside me
Now, I send you into the world
To shine and blossom.

MY ANGEL

My gorgeous and exceptional queen
With the smile of an angel
Longing ears and welcoming heart
Calm spirit like that of a dove
Healing this my troubled heart.

I AM ALL EARS

I love your company
You are a good storyteller
Very captivating and interesting
I can't wait for another date
Wish not to go.

PRETTY WOMAN

Beautiful and elegant
Charming and astonishing
Vibrant, lively and lovely
A glaring soul with a crystal smile
No man can turn you down.

TRANSPARENT SOUL

Just like words on marble
You portray emotions and wisdom,
Like the mirror
You reflect love and passion
With kindness written on
   your transparent soul.

MY TWIN

Standing on this sign
To chat my twin
But he isn't talking.

NO GAME

Across this borderline
It is dangerous to hunt
No game is here.

WILDLIFE

No illegal hunting
They have the right to live
Wildlife, domestic or not.

NO BIRD

They need no bird here
But I care not,
I fly beyond rules.

FREEDOM

I perch where I like
Especially to greet a brother,
My freedom is boundless.

WAITING

What's on your mind?
I am waiting for an answer,
Hope, it be positive.

LIE

It's not what you think
Whoever told you that, lied
I never did it.

HOW LONG

You are everything I want
Please don't keep me hanging,
How long do I have to wait?

SHE'S NOBODY

You are the one I love
Do not bother yourself about her,
She's nobody you know.

MY FAMILY

I cannot do otherwise
My family is everything to me,
Needless pressing further.

GOLDEN COUPLE

Here, is a world
As beautiful as paradise
Friendly and fair to couple.

Let this golden love blossom
And drink from this fountain
Let this greenness renew us.

MY RAINBOW

You are the rainbow
Yellow, red, green, blue, white
Brightening my world.

Hold on, stand with me
Love me real, fear nothing
I'm your angel in this colourful
  valley.

JUST THE TWO OF US

In this love garden
It is just the two of us,
Let our love flourish.

This fountain is rich enough
Enough to sustain our joy,
And this field is green for our rest.

HAPPY MOMENT

I brought you here
To show you nature
That you may believe in love.

Let me lead your heart
Amidst this wonderful vine
That you may love none but me.

BELIEVE

You have to believe in me
That I will love you none,
Listen, I am the real man.

Trust me with your heart
Let no doubt creep in,
Believe, let me show you love.

EXCITEMENT

See my balloon
It is big and great,
Beautiful to play with
It breaks and bursts
Unannounced, just like life.

CHILDHOOD

This is what we do
When we have all the time,
But adulthood is the opposite.
A tale of hectic and busy life
Tedious and uneasy.

MEMORIES

I remember when life was easy
When we played and enjoyed
　everything,
Now, we are no longer at ease.
We thank God for each thing
Knowing fully well, nothing
　is granted.

OVERWHELMED

Poor child of innocence
Enjoying the wonders of his
　moments
Overwhelmed in astonishment
Of how things evolve
Especially from almost
　nothingness.

DEAD END

Dead and gone
Lying here in peace
No one disturbs our rest.

PEACE

Here is where you find peace
Outside here, the struggle is real
Nowhere is ever peaceful.

DESTINATION

No matter our wealth
And the fame we attain
The grave is our final destination.

GRAVE

Only fools lie here
Wise men never die,
Only their flesh leave.

SMALL HOME

The last journey is here
Where we go home to our maker
A small home for all.

SKELETON

My skeleton is what is left
Thieves steal it not
Nor robbers need it.

QUIET LAND

A land so quiet and calm
Independent people minding
 their business
Sleeping forever without
 snoring.

PLEASE STAY

Stay with me my love
Let me take away your sorrow,
Please stay, and never go.

LIVE

Live, angel of my life
Suicide is not the option
Time heals us all.

A LONG WALK

Let us take a long walk
Along the bridge, that we may see
The ocean of our love.

SILENT SEA

This silent sea is deep
Just like the depth of our love
It has no end.

NARROW END

This narrow lane of dark rails
Harbours tears and sorrows
A lot has passed under it
   unnoticed.

GOODBYE

Go in peace dear
May the angels watch over you,
Goodbye, I will miss you.

COVENANT

As we part today
May this bridge be a witness
That our covenant stands no more.

CLOUDY

My country is in pain
Thick cloud raging with anger
Smoke giving us life.

SMOKE

No air to breathe
We are choking here
Dear God, save us.

CONFUSION

Weird life antagonizing
Fears looming up and down
Nothing is pure.

UNCERTAINTIES

Unsure and uncertain
Life and death roaming
Kissed by deaths.

WORLD BEYOND

Here we are, deeply in love
Living the moment in satisfaction
Together forever we remain.

Even in the world beyond
We still hold on for each other
Walking the street of love
   together.

ONLY US

Lovely lovers amidst stones
Finding their way all through,
Lifting their soul above rocks.

Only us in this world
Fighting hardships one on one
Winning game of love.

ADVENTUROUS LOVERS

We are adventurous lovers
Sticking and striking along
Searching through caves for gold.

Our strength is fantastic
Our mission is fundamental
A team of beautiful move.

TRAPPED

This love got us trapped
Hooked beyond escape
Nothing dares separate us.

Trapped by love for love
Kept for love, searching for love
Loved by love, living love.

LOYALTY

My loyal friend
He comes to me at ease
No fear of being hurt
I trust him so well
And we get along fine.

INNOCENCE

Poor little child
A friend of their pet
Trying to hold on
He could be endangered
But that's innocence.

WARM

It's too cold
Snowing a little bit
My sweater is not enough
But my friend is here
Staying together warms us.

FAITHFULNESS

As a dog
Faithfulness is my motto
I always abide by it
No matter who you are
I keep my word.

LIFE

Life is complex and complicated
Everything is confusing,
That we end up being entangled.

HUMANS

An ungrateful bunch
Always looking for a short cut
Never appreciative of old good days

GREED

Rich yet not satisfied
Great yet ungrateful,
Blessed yet unfaithful.

INSATIABLE

Human wants are insatiable
Men always wanting and needing
Daily, life keeps expanding.

ISSUES

Life is full of issues
No matter who you are,
Age, religion, culture, race
  don't stop them.

SHADOWS OF LOVE

Both of us are real
We live and love each other,
We also reflect the shadows of love.

RIPPLES OF LOVE

From a distance we sojourn
In this land of love,
Our emotions cause ripples of love.

TRIPLE EFFECT

The beauty we produce
Yields triple effect
Beyond our existence.

YOU AND I

In this water of life
We would live it superbly
Though we fall for the storm.

EMOTIONS

Living real is great
Loving you is right,
With steadfast emotions.

OUR UNBORN

Bound by blood
We have a being here,
We cannot wait to have it.

Hopeful, eager and enthusiastic
Lovelier, livelier and stronger
Let there be life.

LIFE

We live to create
For creation has mandated us,
Ours is the wedlock of gods.

It flows like a river
Beyond the river of water,
This life is meant to thrive.

THE FUTURE

We are happy to wait for you
We shall put in our best to
 prepare for your arrival,
It shall be glorious.

The future is what we hope for
Our prayer is that you arrive safely
We want, we hope, we pray.

A CHILD

Every couple prays for a child
It is their evidence and existence
A child that will bury them.

Fruitfulness is a blessing
A blessing beyond mankind,
It comes from above.

WONDER

This bump is everything
The reason and chance,
The charm for the season.

I bless you my seed
May the earth show you mercy,
And heaven bless your journey.

THE PIGEON

The pigeon at the place of worship
Wanting to get a feel of God,
To fly away into heaven, later.

NOT OUR NEST

We wonder of this beauty
A beauty that is gigantic,
Lo, not our nest.

WE CAN LIVE HERE

Though not our nest
But we can live here,
And make nests everywhere.

MELODIES

As we fly around the world
We hear songs of praise,
The melodies that give peace.

ALTAR

Even birds gather to listen
They enjoy the melodious harp,
That we raise from this altar.

A MOTHER'S LOVE

As real and hot as the sun
Yet gentle like the evening breeze
As bright as daylight clear
   like crystal
Glowing, twinkling, dazzling,
   sparkling and natural
Moony beautiful, a mother's love

MOTHER AND CHILD

Safe in those strong arms
Assured, guided defended
   and cherished
O what a joy flowing like a river
The beauty of true love so
   boundless,
Mother and child, a couple
   so perfect

MY JOY

This I have prayed for
Longed, hoped, cried and
  wanted all along
Now in arms, so real
My happiness so transparent
Radiating through my smiles.

EDUCATION

Education is a key
Unlocking the universe
To see light in darkness.

READING

Reading is an art
It lifts and enlightens
Depending on understanding.

DESTINY

Destiny is a mystery
Everyone to their path,
A destination that transcends us.

FORTUNES

Fortunes come and go
They choose by themselves
Who to be with.

GIFTS

We all are gifted
No humans are same,
And we see life differently.

LIFE

The more we look, the less we see
We think straight, but it is zigzag
Nothing comes easy.

IMAGINATION

I wish I could be there
There, always with you my love
I see you in every reflection.

TRANSPARENCY

We have to be real
As we travel this lane of love
Transparency is the sole key.

LIFE

Remember that life is deep
All that glitters is not gold
Don't be fooled by the mirror.

BEST COUPLE

Look at them, happy people
Loving up in one accord
Playing in the garden.

Not in land cruiser
Not in jets and helicopters
Just in mere wheelbarrows.

LOVE IS RICH

Love is rich, I tell you
It comes real and raw,
Forget lust and pride.

Love is rich, I must confess
Two lovely hearts, beating as one
Tell me what conquers them.

EXPERIENCE

Love is not about riches
Gold, silver, and bronze do little
Love is a natural fountain.

Our soul is one, one in one
Our peace is rich, rich and great
Look, we experience it daily.

AGE

Love comes with age
It spreads on wisdom
And leans on knowledge.

Love builds on focus
It hears whispers of calm
Calmness that cuddles its mission.

SADNESS

Others are happy enjoying life
Chatting and reading and
  relating well,
But here am I, lonely and bored
Thinking of all my pain
Wishing life was fair with me.

GOD

So awesome that He made women
To take over from Him,
They create, build, watch
  and guide
They uplift, rebuild, encourage
  and guard
But they can destroy and pull down
Women are God, God is real
  in them.

TRANQUILITY

Windy land and dusty air
Hazy day and busy life
Raindrops of cloudy sky
Teardrops of troubled eyes
Doubty mind of mournful soul
Peace, we pray thee tranquil.

COURAGE

Courage, you have made us poor
And deprived us of valour
You left us and we are scattered,
We have become slaves to aliens
And our bondage knows no bounds,
O Courage, our captor is so cruel.

CELEBRATE THE POWER OF WOMEN

Women are god, they are unimaginable
They travel through life like they have the map,
Reading, teaching, instructing, learning
Celebrate the power of women,
They are just so mystical

RAINDROPS

about the author

Ngozi Olivia Osuoha is a Nigerian poet, writer and thinker. A graduate of Estate Management with experience in Banking and Broadcasting.

She has published nine poetry books and co-authored one (with Kenyan literary critic Amos O. Ojwang').

She has featured in more than forty international anthologies and also has published over two hundred and fifty poems and articles in over twenty countries.

Many of her poems have been translated and published into other languages, including Spanish, Romanian, Khloe, Farsi, and Arabic, among others.

She has won many awards; she is a one time *Best of the Net* nominee, and she has numerous words on marble.

www.ingramcontent.com/pod-product-compliance
Lightning Source LLC
Chambersburg PA
CBHW020125130526
44591CB00032B/534